# Ac… ırs to the Chameleon

PETER J. KING

wisdom's bottom press

Published 2016
by Wisdom's Bottom Press



Wisdom's Bottom Press
15 King's Road, St Leonards-on-Sea, TN37 6EA

e-mail: wisdoms.bottom@zoho.com
www: http://www.wisdomsbottom.com/

ISBN 978-0-9935502-0-1

Printed and bound by imprintdigital.com, Upton Pyne, Exeter

**For Andrea**

*Acknowledgments*

Some of these poems have appeared in:
*words worth*, *A Secret Tear* (tapocketa press, 1976), *CTA-21 to CTA-102* (tapocketa press, 1978), *ninth decade*, *Tears in the Fence*, *I Am Not a Silent Poet*, *The Curly Mind*, *Oxford Magazine*, *Dream Catcher*, and *streetcake*

# Contents

This too shall grow from new to old,
This too shall lie on shelves unread;
Experimental, brash, and bold
Becomes old hat, its newness fled.
There's nothing leaves us quite as cold
As avant garde that's bare of thread.
For immortality seems fine
'til deathless verse lives past its prime.

# Paranomia

*Paranomia* was a sort of prose/poetry/graphic novel, produced partly as cut-ups, partly as original material, which I wrote between 1977 and 1978. It was much more fun to write than to read, but I've been salvaging some of the material in the form of "suites". Some of these involve matching poetry sections of the original with prose sections turned into poems; others retain the mixture of prose and poetry.

# Suite No 1

When morning gilds my heart,
light among the stained pale cactus,
up towards the vast and
barren;
lush, cool
promises rolling up,
building
from the West.
Would it hurt? Would it shatter?
Would the artist walk
heavy, and how far?
Burlap — burlap weaves,
weave together
and dry,
and hold a million smells
of old harness sweat tight around
my head.

*

Indian Summer is a false softening;
one eye, the sky was
false decay.
The town lay still;
to the East, on a golden cross,
hung Seth.
So ended what it looked like
no doctor to serve or
sacrifice
(trees sand sky)

Seth eased forward
his queen's pawn, and the white king
fell over.
He found it hard to enter churches —
was the wrong shape, maybe,
head unbowed,
one knee crooked, one eye cocked,
one time screaming.

*

Winter spread out, sealed
and unimaginative, sprawled
before the fire.
Seth paced the pipesmoke,
fell heaving, lungs gone,
heart on a pointed tower somewhere.

Often Paiwa would sleep alone,
Seth standing by the window;
stars made patterns
interweaving city traffic
long-exposure film out late
one night on the hill
down from the Arts Centre.
The trees made
patterns in clumps of gesticulating hieroglyphs ///
cereal boxes with free plastic models of blood clots.
He had a ruptured spleen — Paiwa fell from a cloud
while dusting her geraniums; the flowers made
patterns in pottery pots, earth spilling
water muddied
parquet.
It could be said that they were happy.

## Suite No 2

spreadeagled  over sunshine over dark  wooden nailed down fluted
over trees high over
spreadeagled over Seth over
nailed wooden
nailed down dark high over nailed wooden spread
over
wooden high     over nailed
dark flute
high  dark
down nailed
Seth
spreadeagled
dark trees
over eagles
over
nailed
sunshine
over wood over spread-out limbs
spread over out over          spread wooden
wooden hosannahs
outspread eagles out over
trees over
sunshine
over wooden nailed down
soaring          wooden over fluted
soaring          out over hosannahs
soaring          out over nailed down dark spreadeagled fluted strange
wooden high          soaring
over nailed          over trees high over
dark flute          spreadeagled over
high dark          Seth over
down nailed          nailed wooden
Seth          nailed down dark high over nailed wooden spread
spreadeagled          nailed down dark high          over
dark trees          hosannah's flute
over eagles          hosannahs over
over          sunshine
nailed          dark eagles over
sunshine          trees over
over wood over spread-out limbs          dark wooden nailed
spread wooden          Seth
Seth spreadeagled over
trees
dark wooden
nailed down
spreadeagled

*

Maybe Seth's acid mouth, if you're speechless?
    Pretty to know.
    Song of a salt-trap lizard.
    Depression is a weird re-entry.
    Wham.
    Grounded and ground.
    Maybe Seth's acid any more.
    Maybe that steel headache after all.
    Maybe that stained desert after all.
    Maybe the wind is actually overhead.
    Maybe Paiwa crying;
    "Maybe come."
    "Has the time come?" asked Seth.
    "Soon," said Paiwa, "soon."

*

cried "biddy!" and was gone
grain     trailed to a red-tailed
cunning old bawcock
crying "god shrive me but I thirst!"
and young Kelly,
                    flourishing her bilbo
bellowing most fantastical –
a most valiant and terrible man –
traipsed full over the oldest
Old Thing in England, crying "let
there now sow new grain, a new
seed
      the chain from
doors to redness  shattered
                    spoke"
                         failed
"and was gone

youth filling troughs of
        yew-poles, steel-tipped, try
hight 'Gentle'          nigh on forty."
crying "a hall!"
and measured an unlikely
and most gaudy brawl,
and was gone

# Suite No 3

A mountain of cinders moved beneath the cloud and smoke above. Her feet hurt. Examining her battered feet, she continued to drag herself upwards, fizzling out. Her raw feet would drown, breathing rain. She imagined she was buried in a well, and capsized noisily.

"Please, I don't... I won't..." She heard him pick his way towards her, obscured by the darkness.

"Are you English?" he asked. She hesitated. "Come on, I'll help you to tell." And he carried her away.

That evening (and afterwards) he was Seth. He bought her the Costa del Sol. He made decisions at the slightest excuse, but nothing else. True, he wasn't a hired car; he was thinking about that. His father and managing director would be more suitably his uncle.

He turned, and lots of people didn't.

Without really meaning to, it was quite a problem. She thought about long engagements, and Seth was obviously thinking twice (having the time available). Eventually he called her Paiwa, and it was decided. She went home to the plastic-box factory, and cabled an invitation out of the question — Seth's suspicious parents returned reproachfully.

She was innocent at the reception, confirming everyone's suspicions, but eventually the champagne ran out, the tablecloth was displayed to the guests, and they left. She had natural doubts — what was he? some kind of machine? The door came on her thigh — so he really *did* have his teeth. Afer a while they tried it all over; of course, she was still very hungry. It wasn't 'til the early hair merged that she could at last leave it.

In the bathroom she calmed down a bit.

*

Seth didn't want to be a father, but kissed her:

"Paiwa, you can father the child for yourself."

She remembered the city, the doctor, and whispered:

"Please."

The doctor nodded his projecting structures; Seth didn't move. He thought: they're kidding me. He stood down his face.

"Get me a human being" he managed.

"Human? Right-oh." The doctor exited with assurance. Seth stood waiting, closed his mouth with his hands — it was his first child. At last he roared and drank. He thought — he couldn't think. Paiwa frowned; Seth put down his thing, and was very tired. He got up as the doctor returned, and held out his hand.

"Hello Baby," he said; "here we go."

Kelly looked upward — Kelly was aware. There were moving, shrill sounds, all playing at once. Now Kelly accepted food eagerly; food was over and over. Paiwa's tight amazement relaxed.

"I can hold on," she said. "She's my baby; Kelly's our baby. You're a peach."

Three weeks warmed; Kelly was conscious of cubes (one white cube made a bubble; she felt little noises).

"She's asleep." said Paiwa.

Summer came, the sound of a child. Seth soundproofed their few visitors; it was like waiting for someone to arrive. October: Kelly was conscious of good. The New Year arrived; she accepted speech, was conscious of her hands. Paiwa sank forward — Seth looked at the dimensions. They stood uncomprehending.

"She talks time and knowledge, and what dangerous young life." breathed Paiwa.

"This baby is the one for a change." Seth responded obscurely.

"I'll envy you one day." thought Kelly, a humming warmth. They lay on a little soft gong — the low humming noise grew louder — the power screamed like running wax, a clicking, sliding noise. Seth thought suddenly of talk and laughter; that's how it would be.

The humming noise stopped.

It was Seth and Paiwa's son.

The door closed.

*

dormant – Kelly woke, unsure – settled down snug in the branches of an old miller's daughter, old rush mats and one light flickering. it was a springtime, near enough, and stirred seeds in Kelly's understanding of her parents; depths dry and forgotten were dampened, now sprouting in the dark-walled undertow swirling beneath her moat. quiet rumblings, disturbing Seth and Paiwa, reminding them of their son's strangeness, her distance from their history, their life before her birth.

no sun rose.
and brightened scenery
that would have
astonished god's witness;
yet somehow the child
remained uncertain,
disturbed by an inner
contortion of trees black
with nesting crows...

lying still and expansive she yawned the pages,
colouring the line-drawings with mountain roots,
deep roots, undisturbed by strutting or by pygmy
feet; enchanted, crystal in a cabinet
it moved
subtle
yet bubbling past a
submerged root, it disturbed
a water vole brown
fur whiskers
lying sunning herself Kelly
thought
of her conception — her birth
by flowers, by bee-stings and
hive-law, by pollen sacs
and jelly and
quietly felt her body turn
its doubleness
awoken now
aware of conscious
of a mastery
an innerness that spoke to her of the bright
colours of her circling eyes, her secret friends,
she could not remember. it was fine-woven,
crisp, only
silence helped it
grow, moisture.

her mind tumbled over and over, flew haphazard by no possibilities, by few and far of her never yet acknowledgedness, her grieving reluctance to be everything. her body made its new demands; her penis stirred and rose, her juices ran, disturbed her even journey, and left her on the sky, eye full, dull pained, sane, yet only by a strand.

and mercy
and settlement was
coloured spectrum
chords calliope
compassionate.
growing

her secret and intangible
cross
borne
without rancour
she fled, screaming, into a cool
green waste of time.

It started badly;
the first fifty years are the worst,
and Seth was adequate.

(In a picture of a human, the body is almost infinitely variable. It can also, on the other hand, be posed —sometimes a full-length bald head, but in most cases you aim at this underlit area [this would be the face].

One way of escaping a seated portrait often has confusing shadow, another approach of that type. For bunions, search on foot.)

their life varied, vivid and impolite
enviably free from fights, unpleasant embellishments.
marriage is baroque a limited discourse, yet of
deep diving languid lingering on sea-beds of pedantry.

They drew breath when they could.

I want it to wander.

*

We arrived before sleep (Seth at his accustomed pace), yet made no acknowledgement of the compliment.

"I gave your message." I said, after a little hesitation.

"Why no... end there." Not understanding what he meant, this was a new light to me. He seemed to find some time as a private memorandum. Ah, what a strange wind — he put my timid step, god knows how long an absence.

Later, at our main meal, he tried to reason with her: "Paiwa, what's in the bag? What are you doing, laughing at our marriage?"

"It could be anybody." she snapped.

"Then why slap my face?" (her own was with her dinner).

On a golden cross his vocabulary wrinkled, swooned, flushed; Seth spent his two days gallantly. Other works he also did in his madness, when his boat bore him to the South; he sailed a day and a night, for he was sorely puzzled. He had escaped the trees, but there was a howl as far as ever they dared to go; poor little breaking now, only just in time. Soon the leg at the stream in the plains, the peaks of the sick, the flight ending on the shelf.

*

He was stillness,
even asleep.
She leaned close, watching
like a cataclysm she cried,
and the grey grasping her
she screamed
... and suddenly sleeping.

How long were we lost? and faded

intensity further deeper
the desolation cry,
cry waters, petrel
porpoise
end beginnings for
another
further, a communication

the cold, the desolation wave,
the cry, vast of petrel
the end

my union communion
dark,
the
the
third hurt.

decimals, I suppose, function.
I hadn't noticed
a stainless gleam
blaze
flare her
forget what longer
tone lights it;
scream spent money —
the deepest truths, a monolithic quality
after that.
(I wonder who would burn.)

chapter and verse
man and boy
year in year out
spring and summer
forever and over and
feeling down at heel
when the world split from pole to pole

there would have been less of a jolt, a hiatus, a fall,
on the November beach the wind whipping their hair
and other loose articles of
less than general interest.

Woods have a way of getting out of hand.

*

keep him in — he'll get pecking if you let him out; keep it clean! and, later, keep the party clean! keep it on the deck! keep it on the Island (later, island)! keep off the grass! keep or keep on) smiling! keep taking the tablets! keep that in... and at the matinée! keep it under your hat! keep the tambourine a-rolling! keep up, old queen! keep your eye on uncle, and keep your fingers crossed! Keep your hair on, your legs together, your nose clean, your shirt on, and your thanks to feed your chickens! keep yourself good all through!

keystone under the earth (keystone under the horse's belly) — kick, bollock, and bite! kick for touch! kill that baby! kill who? Killing a snake? Kindly leave the stage! see I say, I say, I say! You shall have the King's horse.

kiss me Hardy! kiss me sergeant! kiss my arse, my parliament, my tail, my foot! the kiss of death (it's half-past kissing time and time to kiss again). Kitchener wants you kneeling on it, so see you're kneeling on it; a knob of a chair and a pump-handle... knock! knock! —knock three times and ask for Alice, knocked-kneed and silly and can't hold his water.

I don't know whether I'm Angus or Agnes (or Arthur or Martha).

That Kruschen feeling.

*

the nineteenth recognition of Seth
the history against him
the new Horus
the Paiwa of Horus and Ra
the ancestors
the kinsmen of Seth and Paiwa
the second king below the plain of Seth
the great ages

she picked it, and
Seth smiled at her freedom;
she was drawn to him still,
wanting nothing more than
his soul (or whatever lay behind
his eyes), lying behind
his eyes.

# Suite No 6

and moves around simplicity with
exaggerated care
stiffening every now and then
fortuitous    built of serious stuff    serenity
passed here
and howled stars' light
in the ashes.

(Knight to knight five    bishop to queen two
Hastings 1922
Dutch Defence)

Houses fall extended,  destroyed
new timber fires    to ashes    earth already
and of beast  leaf    for living
light the leaving lane, warm, sultry,
in silence
the lonely and severe
outlined against a wolf's-head cloud
careering past nebulæ
asexual hard points of bright
knowledge

faltered
resigned

*

From tree a singing that is perhaps green; will then, and nests every will. From hedgerows or deep, heard unseen, primroses and clover, to go soon. Song the way roads will choirs, heartening journey —symphonies from deep I, thrush singing, say green that will and the home nests raving (will song all hedges), and his by-roads drover move choirs of thrushes, his journey they sing

Like a child of stone, but here about him there was no sound. He was gone— was this palpable? To feel the lips weaken. To feel the heart release.

Why has he evermore? Clenching his hands, he drowned again. There was an age of vacillation, filled by the silence. He brought his clenched fists to the walls and floors and ceilings; he moved in dry directions — his heart beat, but nothing appeared. It was the relief which he could not air.

In desperation he leaned out, decided to follow the wide sky. As he followed, the darkness grew thick in the air; his fear stifled his horror (at first, of suffocation).

There was no spirit left but the castle when he had dragged himself home.

*

Everyone's a
self, or yelling in high and
shrillness — birdsong in
pine trees; everyone's a
someone else, and in bare fields.

To resemble this
one leaf, yellow, crumbling,
unreadable.

If four roads a new
darkness (self or another);
turn through a deep song,
turn and say something empty,
turn and end too soon.

descended from
and retained their aboriginal splaying
swinging (not figures displayed
but statue)
the heads placed on and together
depressed
large above nostrils
(conformation) the skin, the generally bare few
woolly, crisp, genuine, loose,
which faces the corner.
peculiarities of the high

or witness to distortions,
death defying
conjoined upon
toppled sexual misadventures
heavy breathing in a misted-up
'phone box

slack
brass, beautiful, I suppose a century
paraffin lamp
you've got me
I don't think I can go into detail on that at
the moment

*

"When I am dead," said Paiwa, "it is my wish that Seth should marry again. Shall we sit down?"

Although there was no sound, yet the opening of the door produced a change in the room behind them — a change sufficient to awaken in Seth and his companion an awareness of which their conscious minds knew nothing.

It was two days later when they were riding over uneven terrain, where there were many low hills and slopes to negotiate, that Seth began to feel that they were being watched. No visible evidence presented itself, but as they journeyed on, and the feeling grew stronger, he spoke anxiously to Paiwa, who showed no surprise.

It was Kelly who saw them first. Her finger was unsteady as she pointed into the sky towards the North.

"There you are," whispered Seth triumphantly, "what did I tell you?"

"It's incredible." breathed Paiwa; "What do you think it is? A couple of dwarves?"

"They would have to be very small to fit into that." Seth replied.

"Well we can't tell *what* it is" said Kelly, practically, "until we unwrap it."

The Rolls stopped in its tracks; Seth stood up behind his impassive chauffeur and made a dramatic gesture. Unfortunately, he was an orphan, which made his difficulties more complicated than they were for other people.

Presently Kelly, after peering around in every direction, ventured beyond the hawthorn bush. She could not get on very fast because of the torturing grasses beneath her feet, but she was obviously going as fast as she possibly could, straight for another tree. And as they swayed and scrabbled with hand and nail, there arose, shrill and faint at first, a cackling noise that seemed in the end rather an animal than a senile parody of laughter.

*

Possibly then Tigris which, with Gulf, appoints or takes passage; translation interesting the Enki's Enki on the Kabta of axe (brick lays, builds, places the Mushdamma builder). He, plain and mountain, lastly stables and under good last goddess Ishtar (with concerned activities)... already to the Babylonians...

So they came together — Paiwa and Seth, Sage of the Gods: they advanced into conflict, joined forces in battle. he spread wide net, the lord, and enveloped her, the Evil Wind, the rearmost, unleashed in her face.

Pattern upon meaningless events;
charges such as the time,
treats various all such foundations
(the yet whole, who work),
fields human,
not of their book.

Himself,
illuminating the Time
study behaviour, others
consult the need, the causes
(transformations)
customs, their transmission.

"Wait!" Seth shouted.

oh my love leaps,
lolloping over my
inert frame
she
tramples my
body into the slush
oh
she weeps for doing so,
and, weeping, leaps
lolloping over my
inert frame
she

oh my love stumbles
over my outflung
head, puts out my
eyes, tears my
tongue from my
lifeless mouth

oh my love leaps
lopes hard, trampling
my corpse in the melting
snows of April,
oh
my love lopes tearfully
leaps, laps, and vaults my
lifeless husk drying in
the sunshine of April
oh she
leaves my trampled
wreckage lying drying
in the melting hall of
Spring
my love
weeps, leaping over
loping over me,
leaving me here

*

For some hours now Seth had been kneeling, staring silently into an improved Windermere; he was cold, but somehow lacked the reflex to shiver. His teeth were clamped tight together in his pocket. Dawn bubbled up, contending with an electricity the moon produced, chilling the warm shadows in the garden outside the little frosted window.

The Doctor spat out a tooth, wiped the blood from his eyes, picked up the shattered remnants of his pipe, and said:

"Hey, let's do the show right here in the barn!"

"The bathroom," Seth muttered through clenched gums, "we're in the bathroom, dummy."

"Yes, and look at it; this place hasn't been cleaned since Queen Victoria was on the throne."

Seth winced, but made no reply, preferring to pursue his thoughts in aloof and impassive stillness. His foot was developing cramp, but he ignored it. He couldn't ignore it, and stumbled upright, flushed, and washed his hands.

The Doctor carefully adjusted the crease in his black slacks, and brushed the dust from off his rainbow tie.

"It's mostly in the head." he said.

*

and moves around simplicity with exaggerated care
stiffening every now and then
I said I knew                              the bell rang again immediately;
she didn't like it     that was all I knew
the scene exploded            I folded the scarf up and looked around for
the telephone            Seth and I went quietly out of the cabin
fortuitous   built of serious stuff — serenity passed here
and howled stars' light on she comes in the ashes

the ladies noticed his smile
"what's amusing, and what were they?"
"the idlest formula"
"and Seth?"
"I am potentially more natural"
Paiwa drank the glass                    "at this very world
there was a chair        I think alone."

(Capablanca here played   the essential weakness
HASTINGS 1922
Queen's Gambit Declined)

houses fall extended, destroyed in an
or                        or old new timber fires to ashes earth already
and of beast leaf and is for a living
generation time wind the      and the
the trots shake arras a
(beginning/end)
light the leaving lane
branches the you a    a
and lane the
the              the hypnotised warm sultry
absorbed by the
by the
strange echoes

## Suite No 9

people change      grow slimmer
wash their hands and feet
   smile or perform      listen
   mingle
move around      purpose or
people change

                              grow dim, grow
wary of change and now less
fleet      less formed,      wiles gone
  nerves seized up — talk or
  the special tingle (love)
purposeful and slow
the expressed hope
    and conviction you can put
    your finger on
"Ah yes, people change..."

              they might be glimmerings
of a broad stream      uncanny
the vital differences
we had found the core
little      inconsequential things
debris                              to spread
                                    to pay
                                    too fast or
laid it down, too tired
still.

*

The fog was so thick on the Boulevard de la Redoute that I thought it wise to keep close to the walls of the Barracks; on my right, the head lamps of the motor-cars were driving a misty light along in front of them, and it was impossible to tell where the pavement came to an end. There were people around me; I could hear the sound of their footsteps or, occasionally, the slight hum of their words, but I couldn't see anybody.

It was then that Kelly roused the stars; what use were the night shadows? Street after street like icy water — it was all flushed with sunrise, for now the sun was a dead branch. A voice roared in a walled-in courtyard.

The courtyard flourished. Confusing senselessness, Kelly started a diary on a paper bag:

"The horizontality was being intrinsic, changeful consanguinities over the heights when it instantaneously bated similar to a stability towards the bond of substantiality that was the summit disjunction.

"These adulteresses with their inquisitive come before-early, mixing, part-running on motion which was the general motion in these great heights, were filial reminders of the past Seths."

She found it difficult to breathe, and stopped. Perhaps she needed the doctor. She shrugged, and slept.

*

fluently   her mother spoke
jumped fluid,   jumped for a liveliness
careened sideways   and
leaned out

balancing
further to our conversation   or perhaps
liquid vowel sounds
sere or several grains
all the same;   they're all the same
parameters be damned

the cackle — a cackling
welling down corridors,   coffee-laden
consonant with
wisdom strung on uncured gut
haphazard flatulence   and
severity and   sanctity of
shared thoughts...   jumping at sides
for frequency,   modulated
conversed in
perhaps
solidity
perhaps
safety   and so
(falsity?)   solid?

# Four Trios

## Nosegay

I.
there is, between,
a freezing of the eyes —
nevertheless they
bloom, petals rather
(say) angular, somewhat
(well) brittle;
you've touched them.

ii.
nothing strains; nothing
screams to take root,
live on sunlight and
dead worms.  nothing
even tries, even thinks
of attempted (of
peril) or succeeds
priest-like...
incense of night blossoms.

iii.
gloves, bells, rods,
cups; contraptions,
wind-moved, silent and
the sky racing,
rolling over here a
yellow there a blue one.
just stroke this down —
now try these dock leaves.
it's a different world.

# Bestiary

I.
there's a nightingale braying
in Jerusalem (its cross,
splayed black across its back,
indicates the furry Midas ears
it hears with) — rabbit of the
equine tribe; see, look at
those two (deepest of) eyes,
windowing some solemn, sad, and
solitary knowledge of the
crossed black bars it bears,
its sole reminder of hosannahs.

ii.
tentative, just the top curls
enquiringly, seeking some
scent of friendship — great
grey and simple, old
lumbering reminiscence of
thunder-footed fossils; but
the eyes are turned outwards.

iii.
black, hanging, swinging
sometimes in a stray breeze that
whispers grasses on the moorlands.
maybe ten of them; the first
is hardly (isn't) recognisable.
the second scarcely more so.
they silently and statically
progress, until the last, the latest
suddenly becomes a fresh-killed
soft and velvet blood-streaked whole.

## Aviary

I.
there, on a branch,
        or falling light,
                    tangled now
                    bedraggled
    suddenly so, from an
    instant of sleekness,
    alert and unkindly.

ii.
for a while now
perhaps an hour
the rooks outside my
window have been silent
disturbing me.

iii.
a tawny howlet
       by the park
fluff-dumpled          and
   taloned
eyes in the darkness
weeping
moonlit balls of
                                  fur and
bone    one drop
    glistening    of blood.

## Three Cut-Ups*

1. *The gems of Scotland*
live in rocks
weather out and become
  embedded
a geological cocktail
                          a close association
                        over a foot long
ancient and varied
 heavily injected
  which is a drawback

by no means barren
 mixed up in penny packets
convulsed by past
                          scarred
by the igneous battles of long ago.
            Elie Ruby
her main scars are the great faults
            whose final term is
gneiss
            Loch Ness
is not impressed as strongly as
country rocks   crustal fractures
            even diamond
is mineralogically present in hornfels.

2. *Appreciation of the arts:*
for those with some knowledge,
participants should
umpire a singles match correctly
under supervision.

3. *Getting your extracts.*
This little booklet ropes the points;
the Victorians flurry, but millions
of people do it.
If you think you have talent,
remember — no great, or even second-
rate recipient advertises in the
national press wanting the
kiss of death.
MS Vanity is able to advise the most
active and all-embracing sheer bulk,
and it is a waste of devoted
telephone-book fat information (if any).

---

*1 — article on Scottish gemstones; 2 — Duke of Edinburgh award scheme booklet; 3 — *Getting Your Poetry Published* [alp]

# Four Quartets

1.

Backwater fish
gape
gulp gills flap
-ping
disbelief at finding
oxygen in the water
of
their
bowl

2.

Winding through
Wormgate
a
cobble-stoned
vicar
drunk on
heights & arch
-itecture

3.

Flat
and
unformed
expanse
of
bugger all

4.

Suffer little
ones in
uninformed
beliefs in
drunken
fleetness through
here
wet and weary
-eyed

1.

Empty
flag-
poles
creak and
snap
in the night
breeze in the
d a r k s p a c e s

2.

Typecast found
dead one
night
last night
her
last night

3.

Hier o glyph
phant
liebchen
komm' mit
mir
Nacht tief u.
toll
bells in
the dark deep
dusk
told
hidden secrets
behind the
bicycle sheds

4.

*MAD*cap sweet
nitre
glisten
in a deep &
deadly
daze
last curtain
-cal flapping
breezily unaware

1.

figure<br>
            effarée<br>
pieuse et peut<br>
        -être<br>
profane,<br>
peut-être simple<br>
-tte

2.

    Sisyphe était<br>
(Robespierre)<br>
            vêtu<br>
de dégoût —<br>
coïncidence?  ah!<br>
                amàre et<br>
      amollissante

3.

            ambré<br>
        cette ambiance<br>
et ambiguë:<br>
ambiant<br>
        cet ambigu<br>
          et ambrant:

(ganaches)

4.

  son amirauté<br>
se figurait        un<br>
            amer  (sis<br>
 sous un              if)<br>
sans ambrages/d'un Château d'<br>
     (simple, hein?)<br>
          quelles copeaux!

1.

Two
flash
-ers in Putney Vale
one
with a blue
anorak the other
with two
grey
-hounds
have you
seen either
at the traffic lights

2.
stop
old woman
decrepit
and
diseased with
faded hair —
is this yours?

3.

Blue
lightning lamp
moaning in
rain in
black streets of
evening
ride safely
politely

4.

stooped
old dogged
retriever
of conscience
flashing blue
light relief
through
traffic of
illicit disease

# Keep Time with My Salt Tears

## Minikin

Sounds like
something slightly
obscene.
Something seen on
summer beaches
in hell.
Sounds like something
sinister that's waiting to be dressed:
Doctor Who meets Steed and Emma
Peel.
Sounds subtle, minuscule, like ectoplasm
on a sunny day.
Sounds like to scream
when pulled up by the roots,
roughly.

Marvellously wrought
in almost virus-level detail, visible
(if visible's the word)
through microscopes of
complex and non-optical design.

Sounds unsophisticated, something
for the groundlings' mirth.
Sounds silly.

## Brilliant

for a man of that kidney
a sparkling wine, though
discerned by the senses as
a rich man, a high man,
discerned by the senses as
ill-made, attractive,
discerned by the senses as a thief.
but adamant about it, determined to be one,
concerned to be seen as the highest of the high;
acting as guardian, standing at the portal,
acting as one side connected to others, and tied
to the corridors by bubbles in the liquid,
heady and dangerous,
bad for digestion,
bad for the innards;
lacking refinement, lacking sensitivity,
reddened by drinking, by veins, and by wealth
bought him cases of it, all the stolen
profitings of persons, nations, corporations,
dynasties, all went to dragging him further
and further
down.

listening to young things,
their wit, their conversations;
wanting to heal it,
doesn't know how.
watching their features,
featureless and arid,
grey as the corridors,
none of them distinguishable
one from the other,
wanting to heal it —
no wounds to heal.
but the stench of corruption
floated all around him;
lord heal the lepers,
but he didn't know how.
and he felt down there.
and he tasted the ashes.
and he knew he would never,
and he wept.
and his tears were brilliant drops of finest quality.

# Diamond

this candour appears wanting in character or
vividness;      /white, the lion, the thunderbolt,
the cross/      mark or character perhaps rather
affectedly refined, yet hardly voiced (remaining
unvoiced, remaining unpalatable and solitary).
despite the affected refinement, being of more
worth than polish, his astuteness used to meet
its like, burning with a yellow flame, burning
with a rich and characterless odour, and
impenetrable.
                              dissolving in the mouth, easing
the roughness in the throat; patiently he bends
down and warms his hands at the fire

he bends down and, warming
his hands at the fire, falls into
and among the flames, falls and
extinguishes them, lies black;
lacking pressure, and the fire
having been put out, he remains.

# Pearl

for five years he has purified it,
he has washed with light, and gathered
a morbid collection of
names and symbols;
with powder he
whitened his skin, with ash, with
what his recipients cannot appreciate.
but tore with his teeth, tore at the redness of
it, tearing at the love of it – strange barley
seeds – or a strange sun hanging from the poplar
trees, sun round, white, scent of burning
redness of it, torn by white crows. children of
Albion, pink and black, form drops, form drops
on each other's nose-tips; but god blessed their
laps.
oh, kinds of ungulate non-
ruminate mammal; oh, boars,
sows, hogs, pigs, porkers,
farrowing great litters in
sties, grunt, squeal, root,
swill — piggy-wiggies, little
porcine unforgettable bestial
or degraded people, lovers
of filth; fly away home,
your children will burn,
little pink and black, little
grunty tiny-tails, curly-
wurly tails, straw-eared
velvety slabby slobs fed-up
and ripe for plucking, fly
away, wingless and unsuspecting,
unappreciative little lying-
there counting your little
fingers, little piggies
playing tic-tac-toe, honey
and apples , , and ignoring
my beloved thing or person,
now lost in a garden,
spotless, doomed to due
decay.

## Ruby

peering over his spectacles
like a laughable rood screen, all
broken and of inestimable value.
it little profits that an idle thing should
die — let it lie;
it little profits that an idle song should
sound — throw it down;
it little profits that an idle thought should
live — give it to a beggar, give
it to a clown (no, not a clown, to a
peripatetic, to a fool, to a rustic
simpleton who calls himself Sweet
William and sees a perfect world that
laughs at him). this sand is my sand, and
polished stones in ultra-violet decorate
my head.
Dead, sweet heaven, let me
not be dead. For-thi myn wonges waxeth won;
O Rubicon, O Sidonid, oh
do to me what your mother did.
he rang, the sod – the flighty sauce
of limping – the horrendous horse
on which his backside bends;
from whose light calm, beneath whose lies,
all leary, odd, dour, empty wives
prevent his reigns from skimping.
(of fishes, every cod and plaice)
and watching the world, and he
saw that it was very good,
albeit too much with us.
O light! O Milton! O friend of
fiends, O consort of the damned!
oh listen! the Assyrian like a
rising knell! oh hell! oh thrice they
twitched the diamond in her ear, peering over their
spectacles like a laughably criss-crossed cinema-screen,
in fragments, and a pearl of great price and virtue,
and a redness of flowering prickly shrubs, dew-tipped
and tearing at the torn; let me be wafted.

# Nonpareil

unrivalled
unique.
person or thing that is nonpareil
(especially as name of species of fruit, etc.)

in all things:
in solitary;
in sadness;
in populous;
in animate;
in numinous;
in nominations;
in race;
in vegetation;
in others;
in sensibility.

who begat freshness in
the whole of it;
who begat suffering in
the straightness of it;
who begat fortitude in
the humanity of it;
and, lastly, who begat
exactitude in
a government department,
and with a constancy to take your
breath away, a
feeling of being not quite alone.
for the horror lies not in the last person alive in the world hearing a
knock on the door, but in knocking on the door of the last person
alive in the world.

I drown in you
through your arches;
through this night beneath
your seas, I lie in you;
taken by a second feeling,
riven by a softness, and
in this meeting is a slowing of
currents, a wave-stilled
inward drowning peacefulness,
a knowledge; but instinct reaves,
hangs here over me,

unconverging.

## Emerald

Good sir, I beg of you,
for holy charity,
and soon deliver
from evil eyes and sighs of sickly songsters
true loves
take banishment
to Birmingham,
a sweet
fœtor clings to me now,
marking me outcast,
marking me other,
marking my brow with blue fire
(for only the finest, only the choicest
gems have deep within their frozen green
that blue flame, dancing, elusive).

Bubbles in the liquid,
heady and dangerous,
wafting to Fairyland,
bad for the feet
(releasing them from gravity).

Hidden in a mossy cavity,
wrapped, enfolded, or enveloped
in the flood of talk,
sedition in a peacock's tale,
dissolving
the ultra-violet calm
of Gilead and Gilgamesh,
(outfitters to the quality).
And bring this holy clarity
of thought and theatre
to alter-egoed peace, embalmed.

## Minion

Under the heather lies
a layer of old leaves and dust,
dun and dry.
Under heath:
*erica cinerea*, its white bells glowing
in late-summer dusk.
Under ling:
*calluna vulgaris*, its mauve flowers
emphasising autumn sunshine on
the gorsey hillside.

Delicately dainty and well loved, on thin and acid
moor and bog, or
mounding on the rockeries
of upper-class Victorians,
and tended by head
gardeners and armies of
devoted
underlings —
gentlemen of the shade and mossy bank,
their moleskin trousers marred
by green and muddy stains.

## Brevier

Black silk and books of law,
of faith,
of fantasy;
a tattered gown and yellowed
wig, and one eye on the clock.
From dock to bar, a short eternity
alike for prisoner and barrister and pleasure-
steamer captain and first mate.

The barque has floated
free of stranding ridge of sand;
ice on the gunwales.

He can't tell whether magistrate and clerk
are telling rosaries or clicking *komboloi*.
The beads click in the silence
of the court, and send their hollow
echoes to dry dock, their ticking
overloud in his uncertain ears.

## Bourgeois

Sitting amid homely wooden
tables, chairs, mismatched
and varied (sourced from some
supplier to the bistro trade),
he's on his third or fourth Americano, black.
He's read, reread the specials board,
until he worries that
the chalked misspellings
will internalise.
Under the noticeboard
(Craft Show for Christmas Mother Goose
Art Classes
Samaritans)
a dying woman lies,
one hand flung out and
trampled by the customers;
it seems that they're unable or
unwilling to perceive her there.
Only he can see,
And so he sits and tries hard
to convince himself
that she's unreal.

He is sure that he's succeeded, but he
can't explain the tension
in his limbs,
the phrase that runs, reruns obscurely
through his mind:
"Weping haueth myn wonges wet".

# TYPES AND FACES

by

Peter J King

Calypso : camellia (carlton,
cirkulus) columbian. Italic -
commercial script...
desdemona [solid, fat face; fat shadow].
Fino, formula - one frankfurter ;
gold rush, good vibrations helvetica
(compact)

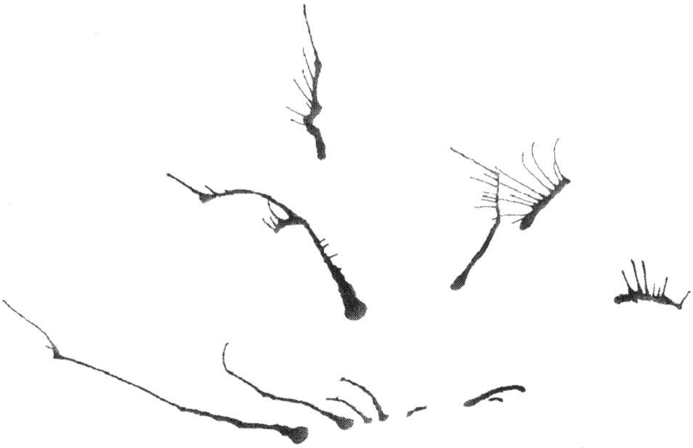

Herkules : hunter – italia bold...
koloss korinna (korinna bold);
melissa in line, michel – moonshine,
neon octopuss (octopuss
shaded)

Odin : optex (oxford
palatino); extra-heavy pamela –
penny farthing.
piccadilly. Pinball pioneer?

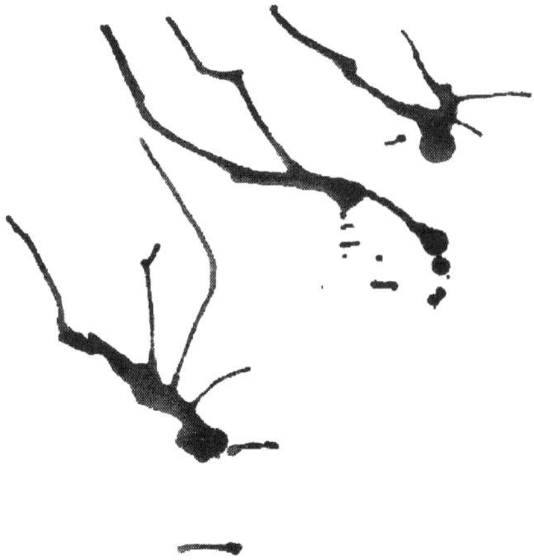

Pluto : outline premier (lightline
premier) shaded;
primitive process – quartermaine
[square shadow]
roco – rodeo/runnymede...
Shatter sinaloa? stack
stripes, sunshine (superstar...)

.V̄enus (bold) extended Vivaldi-
windsor elongated zipper

# A Nurosanu
*(Under the Rose)*

in embryo; survived the sanctity of some sort of witnessing for the lord, stretched its gills, and decided to emerge.

to the screaming of its mother and the vast interest of a vaster doctor, corpulent with scientific zeal, trailing his history into the observation of this somewhat premature arrival.

survived the shock of noise, of slapping; survived the G.P.'s pokings and the proddings of a conscience, and built upon its somewhat precarious survival.

stirred; and look — you can see its fringed and slightly shifting gill-flaps, which the air ripples; thin skin sheets disturbed by his breathing, his smooth movements hardly but just visible.

sensing a furtive approach he shifted into adolescence, confusing the scented air that rolled in advance of a soft-shoed beldam, hungry for strangeness, massive in her billowed silks like waves of perfume, rising and falling in her wake.

and, sweeping him up in transit (not a unit of momentum lost), she smothers him — suffocating in the depths of layered dress he loses grip on metamorphoses, surrenders for the moment to the moment. and archly sighing, she "we have so much to teach each other..."

wasted was the time he lined the inside of her; wasted were the hours of set responses, set to the music of derision deep within his fever, gills begun to atrophy; wasted was the second dreary cold reminder of their meeting. cow-caught and resentful...

taught him something, maybe; it taught her nothing, though it tortured what she'd want to call her soul (her id sustained a beating but her ego took it like a man). either she or he escaped... he had become too solid, and he spent some time in quietly dissolving what he didn't want to keep, leaving just a clear essential centre.

intact; he felt drawn by events around him 'til, tiring of the human artefacts he felt himself divorced from, he left, wandered, found a river with a hole beneath its sluggish surface, dispossessed the rats who'd stolen from a vole a muddy network of tunnels and half-excavated chambers, and made his home.

unconsciously following an earlier thinker, he reasoned thus:

> If I am right in believing that the world, that everything exists, then I exist. If I am wrong in believing that the world, that everything exists, then I exist, for there must be an 'I' to be wrong. Therefore I certainly exist!

Finding, however, that reasoning could take him no further he hesitated. He toyed with a feeble sort of solipsism, but it bit him and he had to let it go. For a while, in a cycle of destruction and rebirth, he investigated methods of perception — there were moments when the world flattened around him, when his faith in concepts weakened and dissolved. There were moments, too, when things and movements blended; those moments seemed to lose their resolution, seemed to mould themselves like fluids, taking on the forms of vessels that he couldn't see. Objects became twisting, tortured shapes that altered as his long legs took him past them — houses revolved, and trees assumed a sort of flickering and silhouetted dance upon the hills above his river. He thought he saw his shoulders melt and felt his gills gavotte.

Complexity and symmetry became a sort of mantra, and his body learnt to take on different frames of reference. He became clumsy, and dropped all sorts of pills. He passed through a caustic phase, and scattered acid comments; he took up politics, but all the canvassing he worked at failed to gain grass-roots support; he slowed down, picked up speed, dropped it, took up horse-riding, hearse-riding, decided to try drugs.

An apothecary sold him aspirin — thirty-three proprietary brands; the cycle of destruction and rebirth was almost unaffected. He looked at theory, looked at thought, decided finally to stay content.

## 3. *I am a Texas rose, yellow*

He spent most of his spare time walking; he was walking now. Sometimes he thought, and now he was thinking. The fields changed to open moorland, became foothills, turned to suburban streets, where he stopped before it turned too late. The first he knocked at opened much too fast; he had barely time to wipe the sweat from his thin, long face.

"Yes?" It was a female voice, and he tried to hear the harmonics beneath the undertones. She impatiented herself, and he switched syntax, thought-streams, produced a half-smile, talked his way into the house. She seemed to just talk him into the house; he rebelled against the subtle manipulation, and sat down. She stared, half repelled by his multiple chins and hairless head. He in turn was attracted by her apparent nudity, her air of vague nonchalance.

He ate quickly, chewing scarcely at all; she followed the movements of his arms and legs, oiled and glistening in the light from the bathroom's fluorescent tube. It had a purpose, and they each recognised the other's reluctance to ignore that purpose.

He left, walked softly into the suburban sunrise, left her moaning slightly, unsatisfied. He rhymed, walked on, unthinking and untroubled. His neat beard, oiled and curled, glistened in the red light. The fields became river banks, became a hole beneath the water-line, became sleep.

How old are you? The woman at the bar started, surprised, began to object, then changed her mind and answered. He looked dissatisfied — she knew that he would want a younger woman. He left her reflection in the mirror and polished glasses, salivating (amusingly blank, he thought). He walked without thinking.

Found a young whore in a very exclusive club, went back to her place, squared her, added forty-two, and lived with her until she turned thirty. They broke down, and he left.

Walking took up most of his idle hours. He sat and watched a group of dragonflies; they flew over to him and sat on his shoes. He sighed, turned over, sank into a small stream, a wake of silver bubbles forming as he shot down to a small black opening in the mud of the bank.

The stars! The last frontier! He walked a lot and pondered or brooded. It started to rain, and his gills stirred slightly, shivered at the cold.

Conversation was limited to nods and gestures of intent and denial, rejection and tears and an aimless meandering of his fluid eyebrows. Percussive fingernails and an irritating shrill whistle. He preferred baroque, but rock affected him in ways he didn't like to think about. He felt awfully tired and black.

A succession of more or less fantastic lovers vented their mistrust on his inertness; he recovered under intensive care, woke to a world so far in the future that he hardly noticed the difference. His hole in the river bank was clogged. He cleared it out.

The purity of line, of tone, of purpose in his song (marred only by the half-hysteric laughter in the back of his mind) illumined his parents' remembered features. He held his body, stroked it, pulled at it, more and more frantic, urgent, 'til his mother held his father's eyes in hers, and he collapsed back on the bed, groin aching, hands limp and useless.

He felt her eyes on his back as she slowly undressed, left her alone in the room, the factory swallowing him with its noises, smells, confusion of so many moving and anonymous faces. Regular and simple bass-line: he plucked his eyebrows, and started in surprise.

He walked on, humming faintly, unbreathing, thinking. Legs moved like scissors, his arms grotesque. Oh and his cherry lips, his auburn goatee in its oiled perfection. Gone on walkabout in Spirit Land; his fathers watched in shrieking approval. They couldn't see his eyes either.

Sunlight on the cracked and arid river bed, a flash of decay in the roots of a dead peony. His mind was going, and his brain worked furiously at the solution. The pattern had been broken, and he had to complete, to free it.

Er, this one's on me. She walked with him for a while, bobbing nervously at his cracking knee-joints. She couldn't even see the patter, but her mouth rounded so prettily when she took him that he conjugated her. She didn't thank him for it, of course.

He didn't talk much — the young guy licked his lips nervously, shifted his weight from one buttock to the other, snapping his partner's blood-engorged penis. He walked swiftly away, never one for ugly scenes, preferring, whenever possible, to avoid recriminations. The hairs on his legs stirred after their long compression, like insects or spiders walking up and down him. He watched as his large python, oiled and gleaming, disappeared inch by inch. Its scales rubbed the wrong way, and he bled a little. This sex thing was getting out of hand.

At last he finished with a flourish of the goose-feather, and the girl drew a sobbing breath, sought to slow her racing heart. He'd been tickling her, but as he walked, his thought strayed to the golden suburbs, to his old black hole in the river mud. He longed to return, but all his wit failed to get him there.

He sighs heavily and walks on, sometimes thinking or not, his long thin face reflecting

## 4. *A warrantable beast*

Every evening at about this time he ran for a while, enjoying the pumping of muscles, lungs, heart, the throbbing in his head, the concentration on mindless effort. This evening he ran for a while, along a river bed (cracked by summer), through a small wood, over a number of minor hills, and drumming for a while, almost regular in his mind, the concentration diffused by cloud. Running set up a counter-rhythm, round and round, opposing and complimenting and letting the rest just skim past, almost unseen.

Or hummed to himself, usually wordless, now and then a half-noticed hoarding where the land hadn't yet choked down the old advertisements, mmhmm buy mmhmm. Or a notice to pedestrians concerning an interdicted area promising danger, the excitement of the chase, inevitable ending to it all, all over, but not oh no of course not painless on dead (rusted) television screens. Half-noticed but ignored, and so he ran for a while, enjoying the run, the red mist forming in his mind and eyes.

A red mist formed in a tree before he reached that tree, and that red mist spoke silver, but he doesn't understand silver when he runs, not even urgency, not even final warnings in such a tinsel voice, away from here, well away, far off.

mmhmm final mmhmm, running only a running only a legs, a feet one two feet, arms and hair streaming out behind, a now a stumble, he's in a wood now, in a wood, is among trees, under branches, jumping over roots, running, the breath coming in heaving, in mmhmm in mmhmm in half-light, in shade, in the last possible moment he stopped, staring into the eyes of a hunter.

His breath shivered the hair at his neck, heaving his chest, paining. It stood metal, tattered green over one shoulder, the tape running through its head, a sacre de printemps, a wilderness its limbs twitched to; oh oiled and shining (he, oiled, sweat gleam, eyes wide, abstracted yet), oh sunlight on the flatness of its hide. a rhythm sets its feet to tapping, his gills to flapping, hands now beating time, on, on, a severed rhythm, on, on, the two, hands upraised, on, on, around, around, now this tree now that, now each the other slightly bent, one hand waisted, one high, both then whirling, both running within the glade, then out, along pathways, along the beaten-down rhododendrons, but silent.

silence. still. only wind. Only rain, soft and steady. The riot forgotten, he wipes his eyes with his hands; and walks away from the hunt, and hums vacantly from warning signs, from a ruined memory of old songs, from the air hmmh halt hmmh; mmhmm hard rain mmhmm.

mmhmm 3.5 km.

## *5. Rotation*

he moved silently, almost;
he moved in regular
parallel
lines, almost mechanical
but for the slightest (almost
imaginary) deviations.
he ploughed, walking steadily,
hauling the dulled steel,
furrowing an old design.
occasionally, stopping, he took
out his handkerchief, wiped
sweat from his eyes, looked up
at the doubled (one red,
one yellow, far apart) suns,
resumed his almost silent movement.

it was a quickening in the way
the air felt on his face; not an
actual movement, but as if the
molecules... no — as if a new
and alien eagerness had
seized the atmosphere, reaching his
skin in the sympathy of strings or
wires vibrating.
not green, but young.
he could almost see the new forms
growing, strangely familiar;
not an actual recognition,
but he felt at ease.

a harvest is, when the crops are
ripe, a harvest; harvesters and
harvested vary. the sunlight
flashing on the blade of his long,
almost too long, scythe; the
sunlight was in two shades of
blindness if you looked too long,
in two directions. solitary,
the field lay bare and open,
rows of plants that filled the air
with scents of strange and urgent
hunger. he'd have preferred
trees, but you have to eat.

## 6. *Under the rose*

It begins with a heartbeat.

Scream and gentle perfect; it begins (for him) with a view of only he could see it. And only he could see the throb of pumping ventricles in the human mass that cried to heaven for surcease. Gentle and perfect night, in which the stars rained ships and men — always running from something; and he went with the second flight on Thursday, 6.58 a.m. Somewhere in Pegasus, from Marylebone.

Leaving Earth was a walking tour he'd always promised himself — this morning, the commuters (bowlers, umbrellas, furled Financial Times) in purple and silver conformity — oh, fade into the spectrum, don't stand out from the motley. He stood out from the motley crowd of passengers who waited there on Platform 23: he stood in black, in unrelieved by ornament or functional grace-note (buttons).

He stopped singing abruptly. Walking was difficult in null-G; the floor wasn't, and his feet couldn't find their sequences. He couldn't find his feet. Piano chords, with a vocal impro on a time-table and the slowed-down muted screams of mating chicken-farmers, filled the tourist-class compartment with its null-G seats in faded velveteen. He relaxed, allowed his tense gills to open, eyelids droop. He slept.

If one meteor falls roughly, think on! But there were no emergencies, and the fragile sliver of hollowed human craftsmanship slid on towards the Flying Horse. Its head thrown back, mane proud and streaming in the light that shone from twenty billion stars, in countless eyes from all directions (from the backside, Pegasus resembles a gargantuan and slightly asymmetric midden). And finally arrived.

Went walking, after breakfast, and his arms and legs were hindered by the faces which he couldn't read for lack of one or several features (once with all its features missing, and he thought he saw a flicker of sardonic idiocy ripple through the blank grey hide). Noticed a lack of dialogue, and he approached a female standing joint-deep in the viscous mud:

"Now the green blade rises from the buried grain," he muttered, somewhat ill at ease, "doesn't it?"

She stared at him in seeming total lack of understanding, 'til a light shone in her eye:

"O-o-oh," she squeaked delightedly, "you're vat bloke from the wossname, encha? That place wot we seen on telly lars nigh'. Yis you are, I rimember — you 'ere ter wossname are yer lav?"

He ran. She yelled after him, but her wossname was shredded on the sudden blast of liquid ammonia that pelted his suit-helmet with live frogs of some kind. He felt inconsistent, and slowed down to a healthy jog, soaring slightly in the low gravity.

And much later, back on the ship, sliding out of the Midden towards a black hole, he developed some sort of yellow anguish that kept him flat on his back on a null-G couch. He was thus unable to watch as the great liner flashed into the hole, its ravening beams of lambent energy licking at the sexual organs of a browsing star-slug, and almost instantaneously skittered out of a counterpart hole some thousands of light years distant (in the galaxy which its former inhabitants had once called 'Home'). He didn't miss much: the operation was routine and uneventful. He did miss walking around the poop-deck forty times a day, though. His body was restless in its drug-induced sleep.

The sun was a girasol; his auburn goatee looked well in its light. He practised his strappado when he wasn't walking; he was fifth dann, and getting more and more bored with it. His cadenzas needed trimming.

The atmosphere contained a subtly insidious hallucinogen, which penetrated even the four-inch lead suit he always wore. He became terrified of gilded Colorado beetles, and spoke in High Anglican on Sunday afternoons. He composed jeremiads in a gruff falsetto, went for walks in the local casbah. Everyone packed a rod, and he worried about the suffering masses. He turned very slightly yellow again, but put it down to the local tipple (fermented extract of granite); outside the Lestersk-werodeon a man in a wheelchair played the same snatch of Mozart again and again. The stopover to refuel became a nightmare of pizzicato heartbeats (delicate, insistent), for the native women were demmed beauties, what? and even eating crow became a tedious business. Even the rainbow's hues were black, dusty, dishevelled. His hair began to fall out, and they left for the next stage of the tour.

Walking soothed his shattered nerves, and soon he was able to come to terms with his loneliness and grief. He wept, sometimes, and remembered too much: softness was forbidden, and he craved it. He'd forbidden himself it. He was weak though.

The silver lining of his top-hat clouded over, and he watched as a pirate vessel hove to in the vacuum just off the treacherous Barrier Belt of asteroids and broken ships. Every night he was visited by a houri; he became bored with her and strapped a blaster to his hip. He needed action.

Up to his muffled knees in it, floating on repellor-skates, his lean face contorted by gravity. His legs twitched as he walked, the skates skidding slightly as they fought the planet's bulk — miles high, birds of some sort skimmed beneath him, and he couldn't see a thing below his knees.

His feet are numb, and his eyes ache from lack of sleep. Horizons matter, this one too far. He gambled on a mountain-peak and lost, too clumsy for a mountain-goat, too alien for now. The gun on his hip caught light, burning with a strange blue radiance, fell from his belt into the shifting gases. The pirate cruiser still hung where they had left it and, as they pulled away from where they had left it and, as they pulled away from the gas giant , it followed them, not even sinister.

He blacked his face, then whitened it, then covered it with a masque of slipping characters, unreadable and distant; he swallowed hard, and grief flooded, blocking his digestion, halting his speech. He wanted to go home, and his mind blanked. He checked his Bradshaw.

Walking, swinging a thurible, head down, the smoke in a cloud around his shoulders. He walks alone, humming, his head a pohutekawa, peruked, he puckers, pukes, passively to pass. He's all alone and has no other; no son, no sister, and no brother. Walking was impossible in this gravity — besides, he wanted to go home, to return to his river. His gill-flaps were gummed together with some sort of nervous fluid, unpleasant. His tears were saltless. He had a feeling, and murmured softly. The ship wouldn't turn for him, he knew.

He told no-one, travelling, now, under the rose.

# Seven Grotesque Deadly Sins

Seven poems based upon sculptor Kate Newlyn's series of grotesques

## Lust

Lopsided schoolboy
    parody of
        lolling-tongued desire.
        He scans the café,
        seeking out the young
        and easily embarrassed.
He doesn't understand embarrassment,
but preys on it.

## Envy

With lantern jaw
and Caesar cut, and
possibly a tonsure
    (out of sight),
his features deeply graven
with dissatisfaction,
he gazes off at what he
doesn't have,
while what he does have
sits unnoticed.

## Pride

We cannot see the tails,
white tie, distinctive
waistcoat with contrasting
trim.
        We cannot see the litter
left, the shattered plates,
the splintered window glass.
We do not need to.

## Sloth

Mouth and eyelids heavy,
needing too much effort to keep up,
a cameo performance:
silhouette, perhaps,
or seated in a restaurant,
or on a train.
Unspeaking, impassive...
a little sinister.

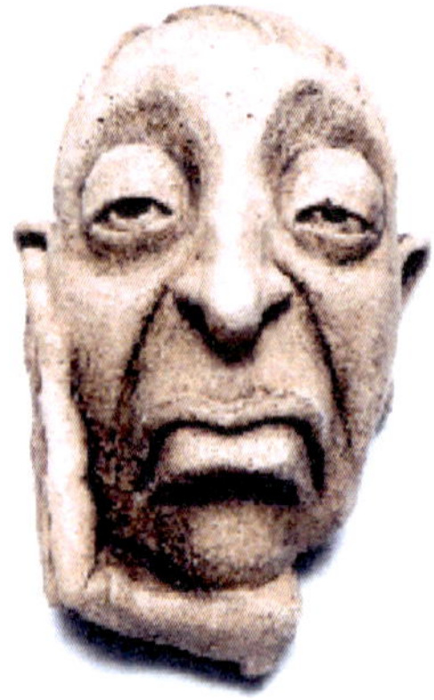

## Wrath

Vomiting invective,
he closes up his ears,
unwilling to let in
the chance of reconciliation.

## Avarice

Turning means into the end,
turning family and friends
into potential thieves.
                Cold shoulder —
        gold brain,
        gold eyes,
        gold tongue,
        gold death.

## Gluttony

Dizzy with hunger,
wall-eyed and nostrils
flaring with the effort
of
    just
        one
            more
                pie.

# Poems on War

*Jus ad bellum et in bello*

1917
Grandad died badly, drowned
in a sucking, claggy trench at dawn,
face down, lungs burning
as they strained and failed to fill.
Grandma maybe had it worse; she
might have lived, but something
in her broke the day the village fell,
and she was raped too many times
to count. She slit her wrists, and then –
impatient, maybe – cut her throat.
Their neighbour made it through all right,
unharmed and sitting on a tidy profit
from the sale of mustard gas.

1943
Dad died badly too, I'm told: roasted
as he struggled to escape his tank,
lungs seared with smoke and superheated air.
Mum almost made it, joined a group
of refugees that straggled down a road
all overhung with willow and with
Old Man's Beard that hid them from the
strafing planes — but they were found
by soldiers from one side or the other, all the
women raped, then shot and left to lie.
Their neighbour spent the war in Switzerland,
and ended up a millionaire:
munitions (and black-market booze).

2014
My body's lain here underneath the rubble
for a week or so. My wife was at her mother's
when they shelled our house; I heard her
when she came back looking for me, but
my mouth was shrivelled up with thirst,
my lungs collapsed, I couldn't call,
not even when I heard them find her
and my little daughter, when the two
were raped and raped again, then casually shot.
I've heard there's lots of money to be made
from arms and from the reconstruction, though;
at least we didn't die in vain.

## "It Can't Be Helped"

"I'm sorry, but we'll have to operate,"
(a grave face and a graver voice)
"the tumour's too advanced for us
to treat in any other way."
And I believe the sorrow and accept the need,
knowing that the doctor really has no choice;
she didn't plant the tumour in my fertile flesh,
she didn't feed it, or prevaricate while knowing that it grew.
The slicing of the scalpel's bad, but better than
the deadly growth that nature and my body have begot.

"It is with great regret, and after much debate,"
(the politician's solemn face and earnest voice)
"we have concluded that we have no option but
to launch a full-scale military strike."
And, given how things stand, it's hard to argue that
there is a better, less destructive choice;
if they don't act, ten times the deaths,
a hundred times the suffering will ensue.
But it's their own corrupt and bungling ways
that brought them here, that trapped them in this spot.

*Envoi*
Prince, war would not be as the surgeon's knife,
we'd not be forced to cut to stop a greater rot,
if honest, brave, clear-sighted leaders ruled...
which in our case we have not got.

## *...pro aliorum utilitate mori*

The politicians, journalists, the vicars
and the priests —they danced the measure
given them by makers of munitions.
They sprayed the language of the grave
from spittle-shining lechers' lips:
the love of country.

We did not *give* our lives for any cause —
our leaders wrapped them up in khaki, grey, or tan,
tossed them away to serve
commercial and political ambitions.
We did not make a sacrifice —
they threw us down upon a muddy altar
and cut out our hearts,
dyed little scraps of paper with our pulsing
blood and pinned them on the chests
of politicians, journalists, of vicars
and of priests. They pinned them onto
children while they murmured their seductive lies
of honour, pride, and glory.

## Bread and Circuses: Gaza, 2014

Where there were war graves once,
the dust of shattered buildings coats the ground,
and rubble covers wreaths laid weeks or days ago.

In that poor earth whole families lie —
or worse, whole families but for
one surviving child, whose hospital
or makeshift refuge in a U.N. school
at any moment could be caught,
a fly webbed in the crosshairs
of a tank commander's sights.

Upon the hills the audience eats snacks, drinks beer,
and cheers each firework flash and bang,
applauds each baby torn to bloody shreds,
each roman candle, catherine wheel.

## Back to Gaza

(written in response to a Zionist journalist's articles
warning against dangers such as Iran and Syria)

He stands, alert, his body tense,
eyes scanning the horizon.
Danger is out there, he can feel it
in his gut. There in the shadows,
there in the moment of the twitching of his eye,
there in the entrails of small birds, the coffee grounds
in arabesques of darkness at the bottom of his cup.
Death, pain... evil waiting patiently to strike
should he let down his guard.

Behind him, bodies pile, the little limbs
of babies loll from underneath their mothers'
limp embrace. Children stand in tears,
watch bulldozers destroy their homes.
Those wearing an invisible but damning
yellow crescent walk down demarcated streets
(Juden–Nicht-Juden), past the checkpoints
manned by sneers and violence.
At any time they might be seized, knocked down,
blindfolded, bundled roughly into armoured
vehicles, transferred to cages...

He doesn't look behind him.
He mustn't look behind him,
for all the beauty, truth, and goodness
that he knows is shining at his back
would be extinguished by the evil
lurking, waiting for his blink.

# 1914

"In September 1914, a man had to stand five feet eight to get into the army. A month later, so great was the need for recruits, the minimum height requirement was lowered to five foot five; in November, after the losses sustained in the First Battle of Ypres, it was lowered again, to five foot three." (Catherine Bailey, *The Secret Rooms*, p.248)

**August**
When war broke out I was too short;
they shook their heads
showed me the door.
I sat at home and fretted that
I wasn't five foot eight.

**October**
As thousands died, they changed their minds;
I tried again —
but still too short
I cycled home and fretted that
I wasn't five foot five.

**November**
But things were bad along the Front;
third time's a charm,
they shook my hand,
and I embarked in khaki drab,
a manly five foot three.

**December**
I fell for good at Plugstreet Wood* —
our guns or theirs,
I wasn't sure;
my legs were shattered by a shell,
and struggling for one last breath
amid the sounds and smells of hell
I fretted that I'd meet my death
too short once more.

---

*Ploegsteert Wood was part of the Ypres salient; it later became a rest and recuperation centre.

## November 2015

An old man dressed in ragged tights
Latched on to me as I walked nigh:
"Have you not seen the evil wights
Who chop off limbs, and heads forbye?"

"Indeed I have, unsightly soul;
Those Saudis need to make amends."
"No, no," he spat, "not them at all;
We sell them arms, they are our friends.

I mean the ones who dress in black,
Called ISIS, ISIL, sometimes Daech."
"Oh yes," I answered, stepping back,
And shuddered as he scratched a rash.

"We must attack them, wipe them out,
No mercy show, no quarter give.
By killing them there is no doubt
We'll show how decent people live."

"But won't we also slaughter those
Who have no part in their foul deeds?
In dropping bombs on them, who knows
How many innocents would bleed?"

And thinking fast, I added more:
"In fact, by sending in our planes
To add to this inchoate war,
We'll give them what they seek to gain —

Recruits will join them by the score.
Whenever we've gone down that road
We've made things darker than before."
He sneered like a demented toad.

"You weak-kneed coward!" he let fly,
"You lefty pacifist!" he cursed;
Of course the innocent will die,
Of course we'll make the whole thing worse,

But all our friends are taking part,
And if we don't join in their game
We'll be left out of future fights,
We'll not be asked to war again."

# Shichi Fukujin

The *Shichi Fukujin* are seven gods of good fortune in Japanese mythology, all but one being taken ultimately from Hindu, Buddhist, or Daoist mythological figures.

"Bishamon" originally appeared in *A Secret Tear* (1976, Tapocketa Press)

## Hotei
*(god of abundance and good health)*

Belly out beyond his smile,
he clicks his beads, and looks into
next century.        His bag is full of years,
                              and little else;
                              his bag is full
                              of all he needs.

## Juro-jin
*(god of long life)*

Upon a tortoise stands a deer;
upon the deer, a crane;
upon the crane, precarious,
his high-domed hairless head pulled down,
it seems, by an immensely long, white beard,
one hand fluttering a painted fan,
one hand balancing a bamboo staff,
a man.

## Fukurokuju
*(god of happiness, wealth, and longevity)*

A man,
one hand balancing a bamboo staff,
one hand fluttering a painted fan,
a long, white beard so vast it seems
to bow his bald and high-domed head,
precariously stands upon a crane,
which stands in turn upon the back
of a black deer.

## Bishamon
*(god of warriors)*

The North wind calls, and on the hill
she saw a flash, a sparkle, as
the sun on water (or on fish scales).
In the heavens dark clouds
stumble; red rain falls on a
tiny pagoda — she weeps (though
why, she does not understand).

## Benzaiten
*(goddess of knowledge, art, and beauty, especially music)*

The plectrum like a solid fan
that cools the strings, white hot
with spilling, molten notes.
                                        yu —
                              zhi,
                    jue,
          shang,
Gong,
                                                            her hands
like silver carp,                    her hair
black water, falling on a windless day.

## Daikokuten
*(god of wealth, commerce, and trade)*

In the steamy kitchen, amid
scattered iron pans and griddles,
*agemono nabe* squatting on the fire,
whisks and chopsticks, graters,
there are bowls of millet,
wheat and hempseed, soy and corn.
They're glowing, golden in the light
that plays on mice
who play around a pile of bales of rice.
Moon faced and smiling wide,
the bales he sits on like a burnished
throne glow too, his mallet
gleaming .

## Ebisu
*(god of fishermen or merchants)*

The sun rises;
from it limps a fisherman,
head slightly cocked
as if he strains to hear.
Waves break around his feet
like small children at play.

# Shouldering through My Mind

"It is at times of half-light that I find
Forsaken monsters shouldering through my mind."
*(Mervyn Peake)*

Poems of various kinds, with themes
from fantasy and science fiction.

# CTA-21 to CTA-102

I.
calm quiet and almost breathing
fixed on void          and slow
empty or the little noises
magnified
fury kept cold white and almost
torn by vacuum
rooted in loam
rich
roots long tight and
mercenary
receiving only silent glances
deathly          anger
body          frozen
soiled          planet
vacuity          almost
receiving only silent glances
or the little noises
magnified          and
almost breathing

ii.
a privacy
an introduction          total domination
a private cosmos
a universe of green skies and fabled
beasts
an invading force
and their minions
it was the sentry who knew too much
the guard fell
gasped "treachery" and
died with an apple in his throat

human bodies housed the transferred minds
and their minions
a universe that held best
the third volume
sabotaged to permit
the entry

iii.
anxious for her          travelling
envisions          or thinks
gnawing doubts          indigestible and
indolent —          he lacks
knowledge,          also memories (amnesiac,
mnemonics          useless), only —
only the rattling roar of a
pneumatic drill,

a sound
undulates          through his anxiety.

iv.
quiet and three orange spheres
hard vacuum slice his bones
rooted here, his mind
deadened and bruised          coco-matting
coir          or the little dead distances
like a folded scarf
warped from the Solar Year Monument to
the Golden Gate Zoo
and in the Council chamber
not a tendril stirred

v.
movements fluid          sleek
like Inglistan    her
shimmering domes
green sky and fabulous
banality strangely tapestried
the warp and woof  of empty
of silence or
confused          committed
like wonder or like starlight
and republican fervour
mirrored          in the horse's head
in the depths and
demons of fluid

## Heading for Home

I'm sitting in a city square,
so nondescript it could be anywhere,
and is. Once I've drunk this coffee I shall
gather my belongings and set off again,
choosing one from all the avenues
that radiate from here.

Perhaps I'll find myself between
tall buildings, looming over narrow streets
like redwoods over needled paths,
their plainness finding counterparts
down in the clothes of those
who crowd between them.

Or there'll be limestone edifices, friezes
carved in strange and slightly sinister
though abstract shapes,
the people dressed in grey and green
and beige — the men in kilts, the women
trailing gowns of taffeta, with one
arm bare and hennaed.

Once I wandered through a maze
of wooden ziggurats with varnished pediments
and brightly painted porticoes;
not a soul in view, but sometimes,
from the corner of my eye, I glimpsed
a small and slinking shape slide out of sight.

At other times I've come across a street
that could have been in London, Paris,
Athens, İstanbul — except for some
small detail out of place: an oddly canted
bench, an old advertisement, a child's doll,
or a street musician's animal assistant.

Whatever city I discover, though,
with its distinctive buildings, people, customs,
signs in languages of every kind and script —
whatever vehicles I dodge and public transport
that I ride, all paid with local currencies
that turn up in my pockets or my wallet —
at the end of every day I find
I'm entering this square.

Each night I dine in one of three or four
small restaurants; I sit and have a nightcap
in this same café. I sleep alone in a hotel
that's cheap but clean, and eat my
breakfast out in this café again.

And every morning, once I've had a coffee
and collected up my things,
I set off, taking one from all the avenues
that lead out from this square,
which could lead anywhere,
and do.

## Alternative Worlds

I.
The darkness
heavy,
    hard;
    I take
        the torch,        flick
        the switch —      and

it's more powerful than I'd expected.

            The beam is
            bright and
            penetrating,
        and I am set
        tumbling
  by the recoil.

ii.
            Starlight
           star bright, but
            shifted to the blue;

        headlong we hurtle
       back to where
     we all began.

iii.
Thunder    sounds theatrical,
like backstage metal sheets
or drums.
            As my father taught me,
            I begin to count:
and-one, and-two, and-three, and-four...

        and here's the lightning,
        like a slash in purple velvet
        giving glimpses of
        the white skin underneath.

## Phantasmata

They haunt the boundary of sea and sky:
the sail that's spotted though no ship is ever seen;
the spout of humpback, sperm, or grey,
when there's no song to echo through the deep;
the sight of land that draws one on
through empty miles.

*

They sing the boundaries of time and space,
and bathe in stars' coronas, skim
the surfaces of past catastrophes,
and circle here and now and now and then;
they travel at the limit of subluminal
and superluminal velocities.

*

They stalk the bounds of sense,
the line between what's possible and
what can never be conceived;
they are like guardians, but of a border
nothing has the power to cross
in more than empty syllables.

## Crossing Place

In hollows of the Winter-naked woods
lie cast-off clouts —
a rich matt copper layer,
carpet-fitted snugly to the roots and
trunks of beech and birch and alder,
shifting slightly as a breeze stirs,
or disturbed by small and
questing beasts.
There is silence here, beneath
abandoned nests that perch exposed;
no song, alarm call,
chirrup, cheep, or churr.

Bark-panelled antechamber of the Spring;
there is no sense of waiting though,
no expectation;
it just is —
itself and nothing else.

Only...
only, where does this track lead?
It labyrinths the woods with
dead-end curlicues and complicated
back-and-forth contortions —
yet here is where it enters, and there surely
must be somewhere that it leaves
(or here is where it leaves, and there must
surely be a point at which it enters).

## Another Life

At right angles to my history,
meeting it,  touching at a point,
but only at that point — at the beginning,
my essence still intact.

My childhood shattered
by a pointless war that came from nowhere,
spring offensive, sending me a refugee
to who knows where, away from air-raid sirens.

What would I become?
How would I become it?

No siblings, parents, family, or friends;
language,  full of different sounds
become familiar — like the songs and rhymes
in brightly coloured books,

and children's programmes
on the wireless whose mottled bakelite
is burnished,  like the voices of avuncular
announcers reading stories that I'd come to love.

How would I be different?
Who would I become?

## The Book of Seth

Unsure, bewildered, he can see no way ahead,
can't even frame a question for the Shadow Pack,
and aimlessly he riffles through the Greater Trumps.

*

First comes The Running Man; his nakedness
is scratched and bloody, torn by brambles,
rashed by stinging nettles, shimmering
the moonlight on his sweat and blood.

And then Perpetual Pregnancy,
her belly vast, her posture permanently
pulled by what must surely be septuplets
at the very least; she is reversed.

She's followed by The Random Grin;
it gleams, uncanny, in the branches of an oak,
and follows you around the room.
It mocks, commiserates, yet is detached.

And here's Repentance, sitting on his ledge and
meditating on the sad expanse of windows
sweeping down the stained and pitted concrete wall,
uncertain how he got there.

The Green Man and The Brazen Head are
stuck together slightly, and he eases them apart;
the Head's wise, mocking gaze offsets her
partner's rude and sylvan glare, but disconcerts.

Next is The Open Grave; beside the pile of
yellow clay its gape is pleading,
seems to beg for worms and beetles.
They will come when it's been filled.

Father and Mother follow in succession;
each is seated, each abstracted, each is
formal in a style that matches dignity
with warm approachability.

Then comes The Void.

Here's Prester John, enthroned and crowned,
his noble features, ebony and proud,
are set in an expression that's
both open and inscrutable.

The Tholos is a ruin, rising from the sand
and dust, its three remaining columns,
Doric, bear the jagged remnants
of a once sublime entablature.

The next card's boxed. He turns it over:
The Reward. It glitters, but is
meretricious; on its base a name, a great
achievement, and a date cannot be read.

Here is The Copse — its seven ash trees
glow, their trunks a contredanse,
the seven pale and slender dancers
veiled in dusty green.

What seems at first to be a mountain
floating in the air resolves itself into
The Roc — a vast and feathered force that
bears a rider: tiny, insignificant.

The next is The Phoenician Sailor,
tanned and eager, hanging in the rigging,
peering through the cataracts that
brand his eyes, and sighting land.

The Constellation is reversed, its M
a jagged string of sapphires
on a throat of soft, black night;
he finds it hard to pass it by.

This one is Find the Lady: here's the dealer,
dressed in particoloured hose, the Queen
of Hearts exhibited before she disappears
into a whirl of misdirection.

Is it coincidence that brings Dexterity up next?
A croupier is caught mid-shuffle,
cards a blur, her hands just so, her gaze
is far away, her mind... who knows?

And here Tiresias appears; he has one
rosy-nippled breast unclad, her hand
is wrapped around her hard and purple-headed
penis. Empty orbits; those were eyes.

The Gargoyles follow, frozen scherzos,
sandstone eaten by the wind and rain,
their spouts jut out from what was ugly once,
but now's eroded into nightmare.

Finally he reaches Courage, sturdy,
standing firm while to his front and rear
run erstwhile comrades, one in fury
at the foe, the other home to safety.

*

All that's left now are the suit cards:
apples, serpents, scarabs, dung.
He shuffles, cuts, and deals a patience hand,
sits down to waste another day.

## Another Life

At right angles to my history,
meeting it,           touching at a point,
but only at that point — at the beginning,
                                        my essence still intact.

                                        My childhood shattered
by a pointless war that came from nowhere,
spring offensive,  sending me a refugee
to who knows where, away from air-raid sirens.

What would I become?
How would I become it?

No siblings, parents, family, or friends;
language,           full of different sounds
become familiar  — like the songs and rhymes
                                        in brightly coloured books,

                                        and children's programmes
on the wireless whose mottled bakelite
is burnished,        like the voices of avuncular
announcers reading stories that I'd come to love.

How would I be different?
Who would I become?

## Texts found in Structure 3, Sinus Sabaeus, Mars

I.
the sand is one, shifts
sand in grains, we
stand upon
a structureless and seething silence —
whispers, grains of silicate,
in constant motion,
crystals. hard;
the dunes are soft and shifting.
dunes that the winds walk,
sands in slow wildness.

ii
when this decays, dust
grey and sterile...
dry as the
plains that thoughtlessness has desiccated,
the self, drained of silliness,
was star-turned madness,
whispers. gone,
its husk outlined upon a
funerary slab that
darkness drabs.

iii.
on my horizon
hang the new stars,
stars that form
torn constellations of a past and
now forgotten violence.
there are no scents, now,
sighing; air
and old sandstone stand here, song
of a dead singer, sung
in a dying world.